This Messy Entertainment book belongs to:

. . . .

. . . .

Published By Messy Entertainment Ltd 2017
ISBN 978-1-9998015-2-6
Messy Entertainment Ltd
www.messyentertainment.com

The Bottom Of The Sea - Octopus 2017 © Messy Entertainment Ltd
All rights reserved.

This book or any portion thereof may not be reproduced or used
in any manner whatsoever without the express written permission
of the publisher except for the use of brief quotations in a book review.

ALL ABOUT ME...

Octopus

- We are invertebrates so we have no bones
- We release ink when we are in danger
- We can change the colour of our skin to avoid danger
- Octopuses have venom that comes from bacteria inside their body
- Octopuses have short lives and generally live for only 2-5 years

We are found in most of the worlds oceans and prefer to live in shallower waters close to the sea floor

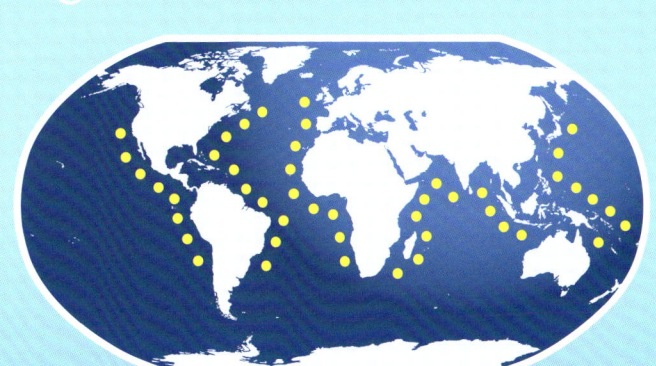

Conservation Status

- Critically Endangered
- Endangered
- Vulnerable
- Near Threatened
- Least Concerned

Octopuses are not considered to be endangered in 2017 but they are a source of food in some countries.

Octopus

Which shape matches this octopus?

Can you fill in the missing letters?

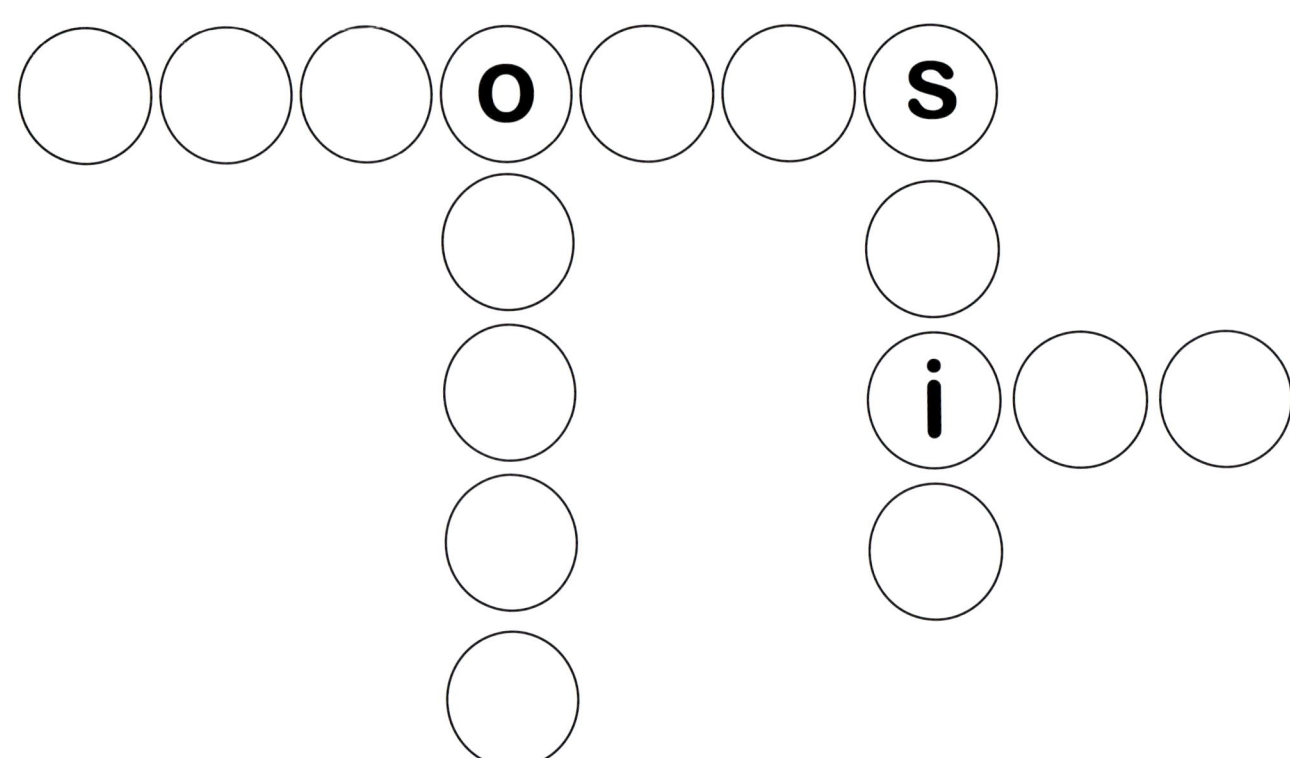

octopus   ink

swim   ocean

Can you add together these octopus?

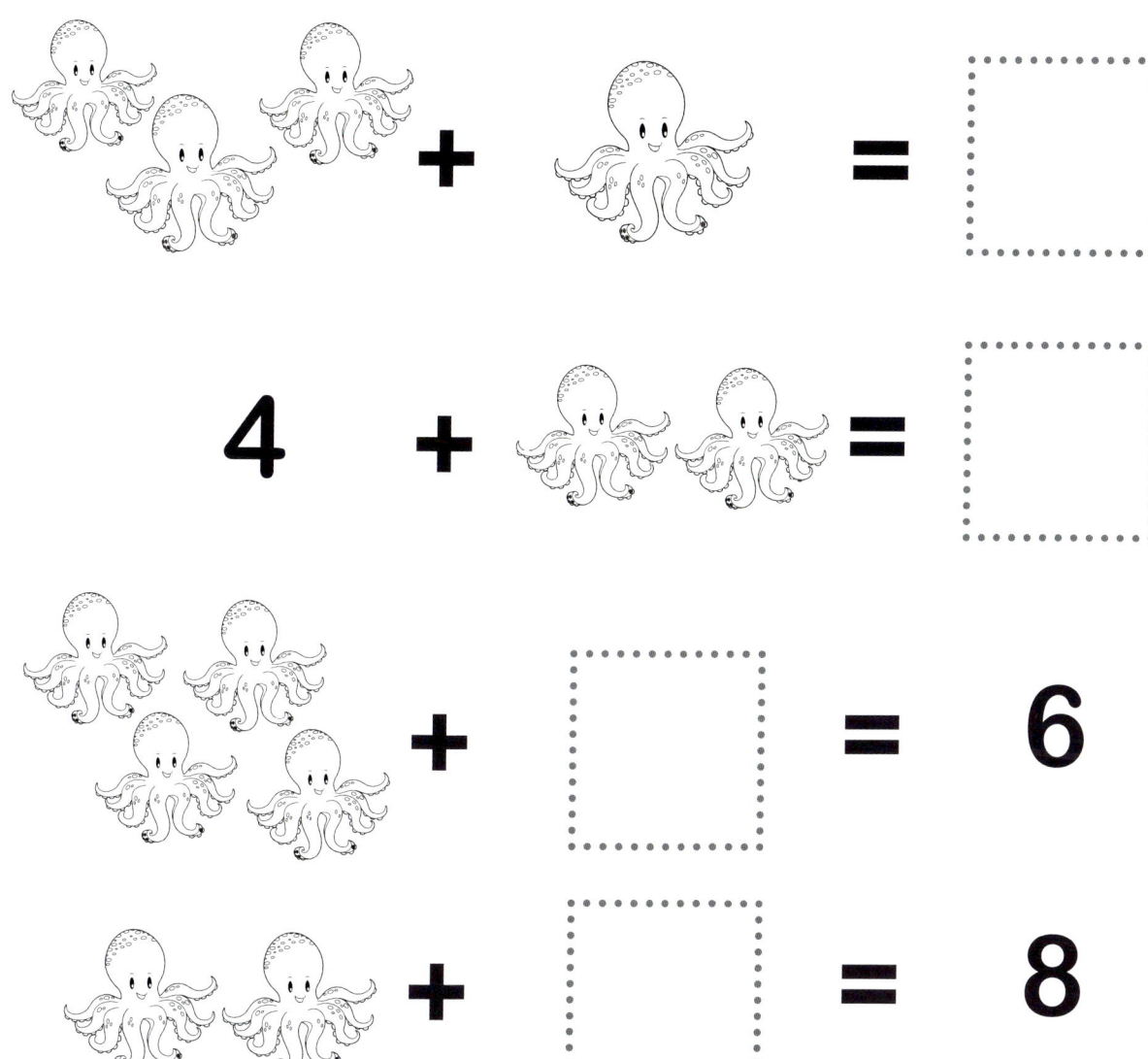

Can you find the way through the maze?

Can you find 7 differences?

Can you find these words?

| EIGHT | SWIM | CLEVER | SHALLOW |
| OCTOPUS | LIMBS | INK | SEA |

D	G	H	J	K	L	P	L
E	I	G	H	T	U	O	I
Y	T	R	E	S	W	I	M
W	Q	E	F	H	K	N	B
O	Z	V	X	A	C	K	S
B	S	E	A	L	V	B	M
U	I	L	D	L	U	C	W
K	O	C	T	O	P	U	S
L	A	E	R	W	S	J	C

Can you fill in the missing words?

I catch .... with my tentacles.

Octopuses can .... really fast in short bursts.

An octopus has 3 ....

Octopuses can change .... to avoid danger.

swim   hearts   fish   colour

Can you finish drawing this octopus?

How many octopuses can you count?

www.messyentertainment.com

Search 'Messy Entertainment'
for books, apps & much more.